FABRIC TREASURES
OF
ANDHRA PRADESH

FABRIC TREASURES
OF
ANDHRA PRADESH

DR. V. SUGUNA SHARMA

BHARATIYA KALA PRAKASHAN
DELHI (INDIA)

First Edition : 2002

Published by **C.P. Gautam**
BHARATIYA KALA PRAKASHAN
3421-A, IInd Floor, Narang Colony, Tri Nagar,
Delhi-110035. Phone : 7153083

ISBN : 81-86050-96-5

Laser Type Setting by
A-ONE GRAPHICS
X-4, Street No. 2, Brahmapuri, Delhi-110053
Phone : 218 3470

Printed at
Santosh Offset Press,
Delhi

CONTENTS

FOREWORD

Fabric Treasures of Andhra Pradesh is a very fascinating aspect of our traditional textile industry and its antiquity goes back to Vedic age. The author has done a commendable job with great zeal, enthusiasm and untiring efforts to contribute to his most significant book which will go a long way in cultural history of Textile industry.

It is amazing to know that this art of spinning of cotton and wool was common to the people of Indus Valley though the terracotta figures of male and female show the evidence of scanty garments.

The author has evolved very systematically the different classifications of fabric based on different materials like cotton, silk, wool and mixed fabrics.

The author with great efforts has also tried to evolve the cultural identity of South India with its rich, original traditional designs and techniques of Pochampally, Gadwal, Dharmavaram, Kanchipuram, Armur, Narayanpet, Vennkatgiri sarees with distinctive patterns. It is remarkable to note that select textile crafts like Himroo Fabrics of Hyderabad, the Kalamkari textile of Machilipatnam and Kalahasti, the pile carpets of Warangal and Eluru gives in detail the various techniques of production.

The most magnificent art originated in the coastal town of Masulipatnam is Kalamkari and this art which depicts the temple cloth painting at Kalahasti is mentioned with great clarity.

The tremendous contribution of the author is that though it was strenuous she visited almost all centers of textile industry in Andhra Pradesh to study the range and variety of Indian Fabrics from ancient to modern times.

In the modern times Handloom cloth has become an important foreign exchange earner on account of its ability to meet the needs of the consumer through cooperatives and State corporations.

I convey my Blessings and best wishes to the author Dr. Suguna Sharma for bringing out this valuable publication.

4th of April, 20002
Hyderabad.

S. Dhareshwari
(Retd.) Professor & Head
Department of Ancient Indian
History, Culture and Archaeology,
Osmania University, Hyderabad.

PREFACE

Andhra Pradesh offers a rich variety of handmade textiles, each with a distinctive character, tradition and appeal. Each region of the State has its own distinctive style of weaving, dyeing and printing. As it is said about language that every 10 kms or so dialects change, in the same way every village or centre has a distinct style for weaving which a connoisseur can distinguish. This adherence to traditional use of fabrics has been responsible for retaining the distinctive regional styles. Variations were introduce yet the basic factors like the colour, design, the technique and the desired effects were retained. Today many of the techniques and design tradition which were extinct, have been retained. Rich variations in textiles continue to be woven in the State. Tradition, however, is too strong to be lost, and there is today a resurgence of traditional and elaborately woven patterns based on old designs, both in silk and cotton in all the centres of Andhra Pradesh. Thus, it is felt that it would be interesting to recount the more important among the textiles of Andhra Pradesh which are popular not only in India but also many parts of the world.

The silk sarees of Dharmavaram, Narayanpet and Pochampally have a distinctive style of their own and have a wide appeal. Gadwal and Kothakota also excel in silk and brocade work, offer distinctive patterns influenced by the motifs drawn from the monuments of the area. Besides, Gadwal offers a combination of cotton and silk with zari checks, a gold border and the intricately woven pallu.

The finely spun Venkatagiri sarees combined with golden border and gold pallu excel among the cotton varieties. The cotton sarees of Siddipet are also quite popular. Guntur, Chirala, Machilipatnam, Patur, Pondur etc., are some of the other centres known for weaving a variety of attractive sarees.

Printing on fabrics dates back to the 17th century. The close affinity of printed kalamkaris of Masulipatnam with Persian sources is universally acknowledged. Similarly, the handpainting art of Kalahasti, where the figures of gods were painted, as well as the myths and legends described, has continued to hypnotize the folks.

Pile-carpets were probably introduced into Indian from Iran. There are two centres in Andhra Pradesh noted for the woolen pile-carpet industry. One at Warangal and the other at Eluru. Among the mixed fabric varieties, Himroo and Mashru are well known even outside India.

The artisans of Andhra Pradesh have developed and preserved an aweinspiring variety of textile art from over centuries of eventful history. We are proud to be inheritors of such glorious tradition.

Thus, it is felt that a comprehensive study of the various varieties of textiles and their manufacturing centres in the State has been studied. While it has not been possible to cover the details of all the centres, this work puts together some interesting writing on the main centres of textile from Andhra Pradesh. The aspects covered will be of interest to art historians, students of design and textile and to connoisseurs of art.

While working on the topic I have received valuable suggestions from different distinguished scholars. First and foremost. I pay my regards to Prof. M. Radha Krishna Sarma for his constant encouragement in all my ventures. I wish to express my thanks to my colleagues Dr. E. Siva Nagi Reddy, Dr. K. Padmanabha and Smt. M. Varalaxmi for rendering their valuable suggestions.

I am thankful to all my family members who helped me in various ways to complete the present publication. My special thanks to my niece Ms. Pallavi for extending me access to her computer system. My thanks are due to my dearest friend Mr. Ramesh for taking interest in feeding the data and in bringing out the printouts with great care.

Finally, I wish to thank Sri. C.P. Gautam of Bharatiya Kala Prakashan, New Delhi for publishing this work in an impressive manner.

–Dr. V. Suguna Sharma

31.03.2002
HYDERABAD

LIST OF PLATES

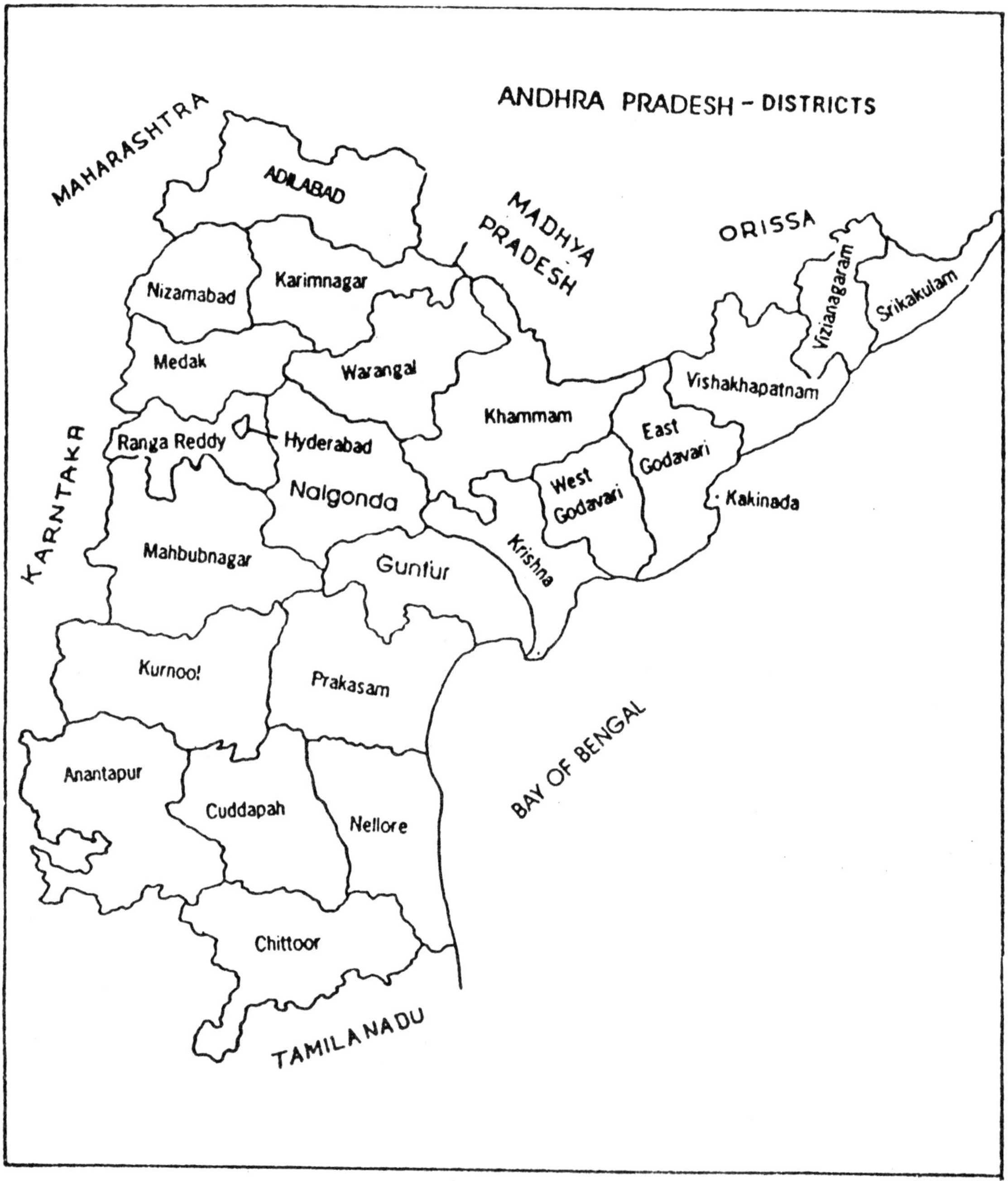

Fig. 1. Map of Andhra Pradesh–Districts

CHAPTER - I

INTRODUCTION

For the beginning of the story of the Indian cloth or costume, we have to go back to antiquity. The excavations at Harappa and Mohenjodaro (2,500 to 1,500 B.C.) have revealed a fairly high stage of advancement in the art of living. From the discovery of many spindles and spindle whorls from the excavations, it may be inferred that the art of spinning of cotton and wool was common to the people of Indus valley. Unfortunately, there is no evidence of textiles of any description except small pieces of cotton were noticed at the base of a silver vase. Interestingly, the purple dye found on a piece of cotton indicates that the art of dyeing was also known and practiced.

The terracotta figurines of male and female show the evidence of scanty garments. But there is no actual specimen of stitched cloth during the course of archaeological excavation conducted at Harappa and Mohenjodaro.

As Indian civilization advanced, in course of time, dress became more ornamental. Dress and cloth of different types have been referred to in Vedic literature. The dress worn by the royalists in the Vedic period consisted of garments viz., the vasa (or lower garment), and adhivasa (or upper garment), and uśṇīṣa (turban) for men. A sort of cloak is often mentioned. Garments of women consisted of two pieces, an under skirt (chandataka) and upper garment (vasaua, vasas) and uśṇīṣa is only mentioned for the goddesses. The female dancers used a kind of embroidered garment (pesas). The bride during the marriage ceremony wore a dress called Vadhuya. Skin was worn by the mendicants, sages and seers. Garments during the Vedic age were offered as gifts to the priest for performing different rites and rituals. The dress during the period, was made of different materials such as *Kusa grass, Cotton, Wool, Silk and Skin.*

In course of advancement in succeeding periods the dress has undergone certain changes and modification. During the later Samhitas, three garments– an undergarment (*nivi*) was added to the garment (*vasa*) proper and an overgarment (*adhivasa*) like a cloak were known to the people of the day.

During the post-Vedic and Epic period also there is reference to dress.

CHAPTER - II

THE FABRIC

Literally, a fabric means "CLOTH". The textiles or fabrics are classified on the bases of the different materials viz.

Cotton
Silk
Woolen
Mixed Fabrics.

A. Cotton : Cotton is a major vegetable–seed fibre known to the people from the earliest days of human civilization. Evidence of cotton fabrics have been noticed at Harappa and Mohenjodaro excavations. The Sanskrit word for cotton is *Karpasa.* The word Sindhu apparently meaning cotton indicates that the Sindh valley was the land of origin of this basic staple and that the cotton products were being exported even in those remote days. Cotton cultivation and its use in weaving originated in India. Cotton fibres have been spun into threads and woven into textiles since very early times, probably C. 3000 B.C. in India where cotton was cultivated by C. 1000 B.C. India produces an enormous variety of cotton handloom products. Handloom is household industry, spread throughout the country. India, from the most ancient times, till the beginning of the 18th Cen. was the supplier of cotton of rare excellence to all civilized countries in the world.

B. Silk : Silk is another type of textile material used as a garment. It is a *fibrous* substance produced by many insects, principally in the form of cocoon. There is reference to silk and silkworms in the Epics. After it reached India from China, the Indians turned this material into a highly specialized craft and Indian silk products were praised greatly in other countries also. A silk fabric is a must for an Indian family, which is used during all festival and religious occasions.

C. Wool : Wool is another type of fabric material used as a garment. It is the fibre of a living animal. It is an important raw material. The use of wool for woven textiles has been referred to in the Vedas, Samhitas and the Buddhist literature.

D. Mixed Fabrics : The abundance of varieties of textile medium led to the rise of new form of cloth used in giving shape to new forms of dress. There are different mixed fabric materials indigenously produced with the impact of imported concept.

Himroo : The Himroo is mixture of cotton and silk, woven with a warp of cotton and silk weft. Extra weft patterns were introduced with a silk weft. The cloth, like Mashru was used by Muslim community. Hyderabad and Aurangabad were the important centres of production.

The word Himroo seems to be of Persian origin and in its corrupted form may be spelt as Hamroo (Ham+roo) meaning prototype or resemblance of features. It is also intended for use in cold season. Himroo was used as tapestry materials, shawls, clothes, mufflers, women coats, curtains etc.

The craft reached its zenith dearing the Nizam period but the demand for this fabric came down later due to several reasons. However, the craft is almost extinct today.

Mashru : The mixed cotton and silk cloth known as "Mashru" literally 'allowed' was possibly developed in Tiraz factories in Syria for orthodox Muslims who were not permitted to wear silk. The silk warp was woven with a Satin weave, which brought the silk yarn on the face of the fabric, while the cotton weft was on the inner side. The Mashru fabrics were and still are also most popular among the non-Islamic communities especially used for petticoats, skirts and vests. In earlier times they were also in general use as lining material, for coats, jackets, for pillow covers, umbrellas, borders of embroideries etc. Mashru continues to be woven even today and comes in a number of patterns. Today one of the main centers for Mashru fabrication is Patan, where 250 families are occupied in this field of activity.

CHAPTER - III

HANDLOOM CENTRES OF ANDHRA PRADESH

India has the largest variations in textiles made from different materials and using a variety of techniques for the processing of materials, for weaving and embellishing. Each region in the country has its distinctive style and technique. Even within the region there are variations in style of weaving and designs that have been retained because of distinctive cultural traditions. The textile traditions were not only greatly influenced by the geo-climatic condition but also by the socio-cultural traditions of the areas and absorption of the influences of migration of many ethnic groups into India, by land and by sea.

The textiles of Andhra Pradesh and the entire south India at large, have retained their traditional designs and techniques, for the external influences were not as dominant here as in other parts of the county. Variations were introduced yet the basic sense of design, the use of colour, the balance between the technique and the desired effect were retained. As it is said about language that every 10 km. dialects change, in the same way every village or centre in Andhra Pradesh has a distinct style for weaving. This adherence to traditional use of fabrics has been responsible for retaining the distinctive regional styles.

Andhra Pradesh has a well developed textile industry, which includes the spinning and processing sectors. Andhra Pradesh has been producing good quality textiles not only the cottons and silks but also fabrics made of mixed cotton and silk like the Himroo and Mashru variety. Walk into any hotel in the State, you are welcomed by a magnificent *Kalamkari* wall *Painting*. Kalamakari is undoubtedly the most popular art form of the Andhra Pradesh though many other arts and crafts co-exsit. The art, which originated in the coastal town of Machilipatnam, later spread to the temple town Sri Kalahasti.

Pochampally fabrics, especially the Pochampally silk sarees [Plate No. 1, 2, 3, 4] are held in high esteem and figure prominently in social and religious ceremonies.

The *Gadwal* sarees [Plate No. 5] are a combination of silk border and pallu with a cotton body. This technique was used only in the rich gold brocaded sarees made for weddings or for offering to the temple.

The finest known examples of pure silk sarees in the State are from *Dharmavaram*. Besides weaving the *Dharmavaram* silk sarees [Plate No. 6] the weavers of the region have taken up weaving of Kanchipuram silk sarees [Plate No. 7, 8] with contrasting colours typical of the silk sarees woven in Tamilnadu. Today in Andhra Pradesh there is an amazing range of finely woven silk of Arni, Puddukottai, Armur, Narayanpet, Siddipet, Sangareddy, Peddapuram, Wanaparti, Panduru and Patur. [Plate Nos. 9, 10], Sangareddy and Puddukottai wove sarees similar to those of Tamilnadu, while the Naryanpet sarees of silk and cotton were typical of the Maharashtrian style. Their check pattern solid border sarees are noted for their superior workmanship and are largely exported to various parts of the country and abroad.

Andhdra Pradesh was known for its very fine cotton weaves and Ganjam district has woven these from ancient times. The silk was later transferred to the weaving of *Khadi.* Another fine quality weaving in cotton came from Venkatagiri [Plate No. 12]. The inlay technique known as the *Jamdani* was used in cotton weaves of *Venkatagiri.* Checks and stripes are the most distinctive patterns used in a *Venkatagiri* saree.

The technique of *'Ikat'* was known in the area from very early times. The technique is used in the borders of sarees woven in many centres, spread all over the Deccan. Telia rumals with *ikat* patterns in maroon, white and black were traditionally worn by the men in Andhra Pradesh. The cloth was initially woven in Chirala and was later introduced into Pochampally. Telia rumals were exported to the Gulf countries, to Africa and Iran, with the weavers creating patterns suited for different markets.

Certain styles of textile were developed in the Deccan, which were especially distinctive. One such was the Himroo, a mixture of cotton and silk, woven with a warp of cotton, weft of silk. Extra weft patterns were introduced with a silk weft. Muslim community used the cloth, like Mashru. Though Aurangabad was the original home, Hyderabad also became a famous center for Himroo weaving.

There are two centers in Andhra pradesh noted for the woollen Pile carpets, viz. *Eluru* and *Warangal.* Pile carpets were probably introduced into India from Iran. In Warangal the Pile carpets industry was introduced by some Muslim Nawabs of the place for no other reason but the availability of the chief raw material, namely, wool and the demand for the pile carpets from the luxury loving Nawabs. It is well known that during the time of Golconda rulers there was free intercourse of trade and culture between this part of the State and the Middle Eastern countries.

CHAPTER - IV

PRODUCTION TECHNIQUE

The production of cloth in the artisan industry in Andhra Pradesh goes back to several years and the industry till late 18th century was an active and alive one. The producer and the trading community formed the backbone of the industry. Craftsmen working in their homes with comparatively simple tools creating sophisticated products supplied the different items required in daily use by the people of all classes of the society. The industry provided employment to several artisans at each stage, from the growing of cotton through the ginning , carding and spinning, the warping, sizing and weaving up to dyeing, bleaching, printing, finishing and finally the trading of the cloth. Each of the stages builts into a speciality craft around which specific communities acquired mastery.

This chapter is an attempt to study and examine the various technical aspects involved in creating the select textile craft viz. the Himroo fabrics of Hyderabad; the Kalamkari textiles of Machilipatnam and Kalahasti; and the Pile carpets of Warangal and Eluru. Also, it is attempted to give some account of the techniques of production. The fabrics/textiles covered in the present chapter are only a few of the several renowned and beautiful fabrics that Andhra Pradesh is famous for.

A. Himroo Fabrics Of Hyderabad

'Himroo' is a fabric of intricate weave. In appearance it looks more like silk but it is basically made of cotton warp and silk, or artificial silk or rayon weft. The word 'Himroo' seems to be of Persian origin meaning 'Prototype' or 'of similar resemblance or features' The basic cotton material is interwoven with designs in silk thread of many shades. This rich multi-coloured and designed cloth is ornamental with traditional motifs comprising of flowers, creepers, birds, fruits etc. [Plate No. 13].

Aurangabad is the hometown of this famous mixed fabric. The craft gradually migrated to Hyderabad. In Hydrabad the craft reached its zenith during the Nizam rule. It is the city's oldest fabrics and the Nizam's gift to the world of textiles. Though Aurangabad was the hometown for Himroo about 5000 families migrated to the city and settled down here to make Himroo cloth for the royal family. Princess Durru Shewar, the daughter-in-law of the Nizam, placed order for Himroo cloth worth Rs. 20,000, just to decorate the palace, shows the patronage enjoyed by the craft. Since orders were placed regularly from the royal palace for the Himroo fabric, the Nizam's government took positive steps to help developing of this craft.

After the reorganization of the States, the Andhra Pradesh government evinced keen interest in the craft wanted to implant it in its own territories. This has resulted in migration of some artisans from Aurangabad to Hyderabad where they got looms and started manufacturing this fabric.

Manufacturing Process

A workshop of Himroo cloth requires the following set of tools and implements.

1. Loom with all its parts including wooden frame, weaver's beam, pedals, phani (reed) and heddles.

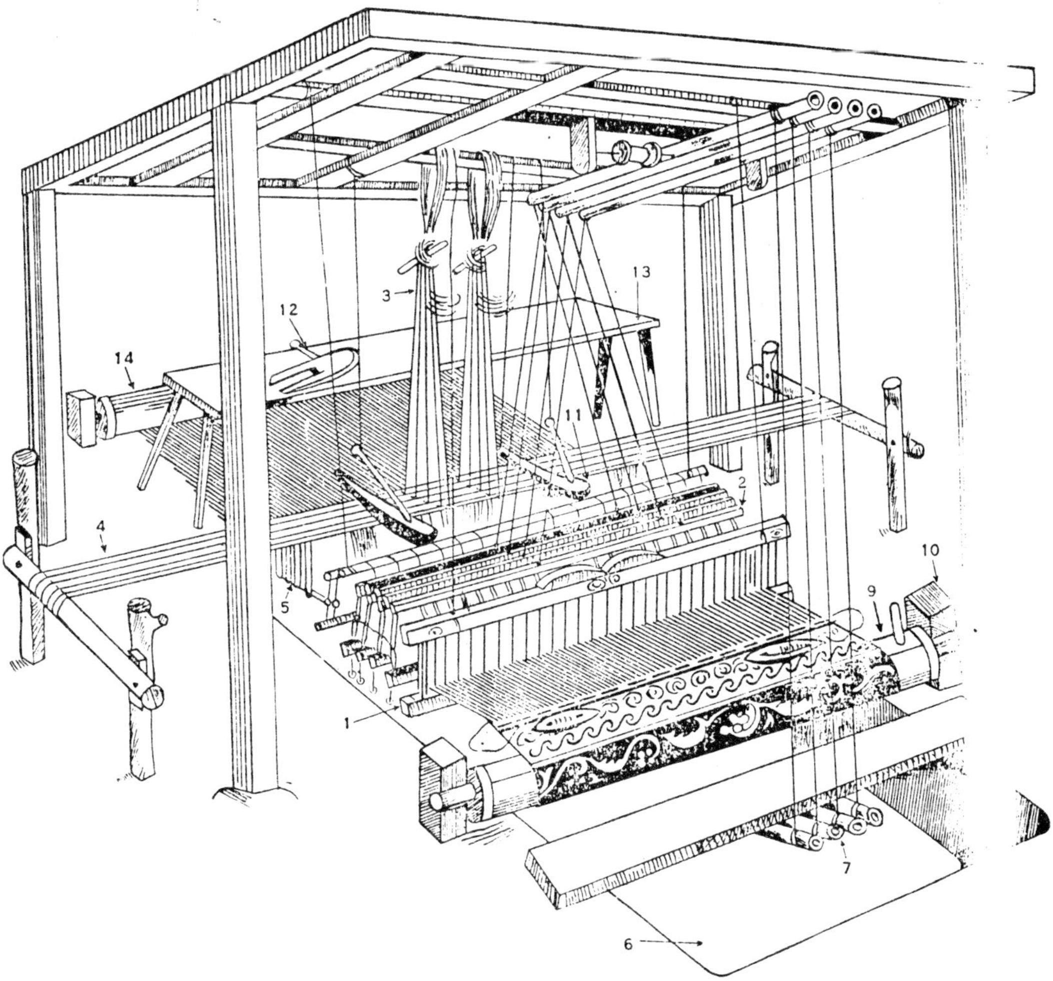

1. REED (PHANI)
2. HEDDLES
3. JAALA THREADS
4. PAGA THREADS
5. NAKA THREADS
6. PIT
7. PEDALS
8. WEAVER'S SEAT
9. WEAVER'S BEAM
10. SILOT
11. WOODEN PLOUGH (ANKHDA)
12. AMBUDA
13. HELPER BOY'S SEAT
14. WARPER'S BEAM

Fig. 2. HIMROO LOOM

2. Katla (Throw shuttle)
3. Akoda (Wooden plough for holding the Jala threads in position)
4. Ambuda (V shape hook for lifting Jala threads)
5. Warp bobbins
6. Kandi (weft bobbins)
7. Winding Charka
8. Warping Charka.

The loom [Fig. 2] used in Himroo weaving is the simple "Throw shuttle loom." The various processes which are involved in the manufacture of a piece of Himroo cloth begin with the dyeing of yarn; winding of the yarn on to the bobbins; preparation of the warp thread; heddle knitting, the process in which the warp threads are passed through the loops in the heddles and then through the reeds. This process is called 'denting'. The next stage is the weft preparation. The last process is that of weaving which comprises interlacing the weft yarn with the warp yarns at right angles. Two persons are required in weaving of Himroo cloth, one to do the weaving and another, a helper boy, who is supposed to sit on a bench above the loom and to lift up the Jala threads as and when required.

The articles produced in this craft are mostly shawls. The nobles of Golconda court originally used the Himrus as 'Achkans'. These fabrics are also used for door and window curtains, pillow covers, tunics, skirts, dressing gowns, ladies blouse pieces etc. [Plate No.14]

Popular Designs

The various designs created by the craftsmen comprise of

geometrical ones; popular fruits; flowers; creepers; birds and animals etc. which augment the appeal of cloth with the beauty and ornamentation. The names of the designs are usually related with the motif that is brought out on the cloth. For example, the Jaldar Khairi, Guldasta, Jungle-ki-Rani etc.

There was a gradual decline of this craft. The demand for this fabric slowly came down due to several reasons. The main reasons being the hard work and less returns involved in weaving this fabric. Next, the production of monotonous design. After the closure of the State-sponsored looms, even skilled craftsmen joined government offices as non-skilled labourers.

Today the art is almost extinct, except for a few patrons who are still contributing for the revival of this age old craft with the help of few artisan families. Patrons of this art opine that its not the government but some philanthropists who should try and revive this traditional craft before it vanishes into oblivion.

B. Kalamkari Textiles

Kalamkari is undoubtedly the most popular art form of Andhra Pradesh. Though many other arts and crafts co-exist, it seems Kalamkari takes the prominent place for all the tourists visiting the State. The two famous centres for painted and printed textiles are Masulipatnam and Kalahasti in the eastern parts of Andhra Pradesh. The art, which originated in the coastal town of Masulipatnam, later spread and in fact, has settled down in the temple town, Sri Kalahasti. Here the art form is still making its presence felt.

Kalamkari Temple cloth Painting at Kalahasti

Kalahasti, situated on the bank of river Swarnamukhi is a pilgrim centre where a very imposing temple devoted to Lord Kalahasteswara is located. In this place of religious importance arose the industry of Kalamkari temple cloth painting. Here the figures of gods were painted as well as the myths and legends described. Kalahasti and its surroundings were under the control of the zamindars. The religious importance of the place and the patronage of the zamindars must have undoubtedly proved propitious for the development of the industry here.

The Kalahasti temple cloth painting and printing is done entirely by Kalamkari process, i.e., with the help of Kalam or pen. The designs, which consist of mythological human figures, flower border designs etc., are all drawn free hand with a Kalam.

Chief raw material and equipment needed are as follows:

1. Gadha or Kora cloth (cloth woven with unbleached yarn).
2. Vegetables dyes.
3. Alum
4. Tender Myrobalans (dried)
5. Buffalo Milk
6. Charcoal
7. Kalams or Pens made of split bamboo
8. Large copper vessel
9. Flowing water etc.

Process of Production :

The process begins with the preparation of cloth for taking the outline. For this a thick Gadha or Kora cotton cloth of the required size is taken and washed well in flowing water to remove the starch. The Swarnamukhi River that skirts Kalahasti town is obviously suitable for the purpose. The cloth is then soaked in myrobalan solution prepared from dried tender myrobalans. Sometimes buffalo milk is added to the solution which helps to prevent the spreading or clotting of colour when applied later to the mordant cloth. This immersion in the myrobalan solution is necessary in order to enable the black dye to become permanently fixed in the fibres of the cloth. The cloth dipped in the myrobalan solution has a yellow appearance and is ready to take the black dye. After the cloth is dried it is spread on a long low wooden bench to enable the artist to squat down with the bench in front of him at a convenient height. The Kalamkari artist then proceeds to draw on the cloth the outlines of the figures and designs with charcoal sticks made of tamarind twigs. Over this the artist draws the final lines with a black solution called the *Kasam.* The Kasam or black dye is prepared from molasses and palmyrah jaggery (proportion 1:2) dissolved in water. Iron filings are put in this solution and allowed to ferment for 15 days. The resultant liquid is Kasam.

The artist makes use of an ingeniously made pen or Kalam in drawing the outlines. An expert artist draws the picture free hand straightway with the Kalam. The artist is able to maintain correct proportions of the body and limbs of the figures and also dimities their expression and action beautifully.

The above described process is almost similar to the one adopted by the Kalamkari cloth printing industry at Masulipatnam, except that in respect of Masulipatnam work outline printing in black with the Kasam is done by means of engraved wooden block not by freehand drawing. In the preparation of Masulipatnam black dye (Kasam) gum is added to it so that can be used in a paste consistency for block printing on cloth.

After the outlines of the panels and the design are drawn, the next stage for the craftsman is to proceed to give the cloth its background colours, namely, red. The general background of almost all the temples cloth produced here is red. Besides the general background some of the figures themselves may also have to be given a red or pink colour. Whenever red colour is needed on the cloth, the workman paints over those areas with an alum solution.

The solution is kept in an enamel mug and the cloth is spread over a woollen blanket and the craftsman applies the solution to the cloth with the help of another type of Kalam, which has a brush like end. The cloth is then washed in flowing water and dried in the sun before it is dyed red. The process of red colour dyeing is interesting. Pure vegetable colours are used for the red dye.

The various substances used for making the red dye are powdered and mixed in equal quantities. Then the mixture is put in water in a big copper, brass or pottery vessel along with the cloth and boiled for 1 or 2 hours.

In order that the colour of the figures may not be identical and get completely merged with the colour of the background thus rendering the figures indistinct, the craftsman uses a skilful process of 'differential dyeing' i.e., the general background requiring deep red colour is put through the process of red colouring twice i.e., application of alum solution and boiling in red dye. In respect of the figures which should take only light red, the application of alum is done only once and the figures get only one coating, thus rendering them distinct from the background, which is deep red.

The next stage is bleaching process, which is quite interesting. The bleaching process goes on for a week continuously i.e., the cloth is washed in sheep dung at night and dried on river bed during the day, at the end of which activity the cloth retains the red colour only in those areas originally covered by the alum solution, while the rest is rendered white. Now the figures on the design are ready to take other colours that are needed. There is no definite convention about what particular colours the different figures should have, the colour scheme generally is as follows : female figures are usually yellow, Devatas are depicted in blue; Rakshasas in red and green, and some figures are left without any colouring at all.

After the bleaching process, the cloth is dipped in milk solution. This helps in applying the colour only to the areas required.

It prevents the running of one dye colour into the other dyed areas. The first colour to be applied is yellow, especially the female figures are generally dyed yellow. The yellow colour is also applied to depict the jewellery on the figures. In order to fix this yellow colour, the areas requiring it are first painted over with alum solution in which mango bark is soaked. The cloth is then washed in flowing water and dried. The application of blue and green colour is then undertaken. But before this, the cloth is once again soaked in the milk solution and is then ready for the next colouring process. The blue colour is prepared with a solution of indigo mixed with little alum. This is applied with a bamboo Kalam whenever blue is needed. In those areas, where green is required the yellow dye colour is applied before hand and over this blue is applied, thus changing the yellow colour into a beautiful soft green.

The cloth is finally washed in flowing water and then dried. The final product is ready.

Design Themes

As already mentioned, Kalahasti specializes in producing temple cloth paintings used as canopies over the idols during festive celebrations or as panels to hang on the walls to provide a background for religious functions. The themes adopted for the designs are usually from the Epics and the Puranas. Some of them are:

1. Dhurva Vijayam
2. Daksha Yagnam
3. Dasavataram
4. Sitarama Kalyanam
5. Sampoorna Ramayanam
6. Venkateshwara Charitam
7. Mahabharata-Virataparvam.

The panels usually have attractive and decorative borders within which the scenes are contained. The artist explains briefly and clearly what each scene represents.

It is a matter of great satisfaction that the quality of the traditional temple cloth designs now produced is in no way inferior to those produced decades ago.

Kalamkari Cloth Printing of Masulipatnam

The 'Chintz and Calicos' of Masulipatnam have received world-wide recognition and occupied a place of pride amongst the Indian textile products from the earliest time. It is believed that the handprint cloth of Masulipatnam was popular with the ancient Greeks even before Christ. It is obvious that Masulipatnam port was one of the well-known ports of the ancient sea routes of the world form where extensive trade in the dyed cloth was carried on.

The historical town of Masulipatnam lies on the eastern coast of Andhra Pradesh along the Bay of Bengal. Masulipatnam is a corrupted form of Machilipatnam meaning a port. A few centuries ago the city should have been buzzing with activity, the town being occupied by the craftsmen who produced the world famous hand printed cloth which found a ready market every where. The craftsmen produced various types of printed material which comprised of canopies with special mythological designs for the Hindus, the prayer carpets for the Mohammedans with their typical middle-eastern designs, the tent lining cloth which was a favourite with the Persian rulers, The chintz i.e., small printed design on cloth with special designs to suit the taste of the Westerners, table cloths and curtains printed in most attractive colours and designs, sarees and dhotis to meet the needs of the local consumers. The demand for these textiles was universal and the craftsmen excelled in their art to satisfy the tastes of one and all. Thus the calico printing and dyeing industry of Masulipatnam held an undaunted sway till about the middle of the 18th century.

The Kalamkari specimens of Masulipatnam are firstly block printed and then the colours are painted with a Kalam. The Kalamkari Industry of Masulipatnam claims that the dyes used are all of pure vegetable origin which are said to give strength to the cloth unlike the chemical dyes which adversely affect the texture of cloth. It is also believed that the vegetable dyes became brighter and brighter at each wash.

The chief *Raw materials* and *Implements used* in manufacturing a Masulipatnam Kalamkari painting are as the following:

1. The base on which Kalamkari printing and dyeing is carried on Kora (unbleached) cloth.
2. Vegetable dyes.
3. The workbenches, which enable the worker to squat by its side and attend to block printing work.
4. A three–legged low table for wax processing and other colour dyeing.
5. Printing Blocks
6. Stamping pads to hold the dye for block printing.
7. Kalams [Fig. 3]
8. Bees wax.

The rest of the materials are the same as the ones used by the Kalahasti Kalamkari artisans.

Manufacturing Process :

The Masulipatnam Kalamkari printing process involves a series of long and complicated operations, which fall under six main heads :

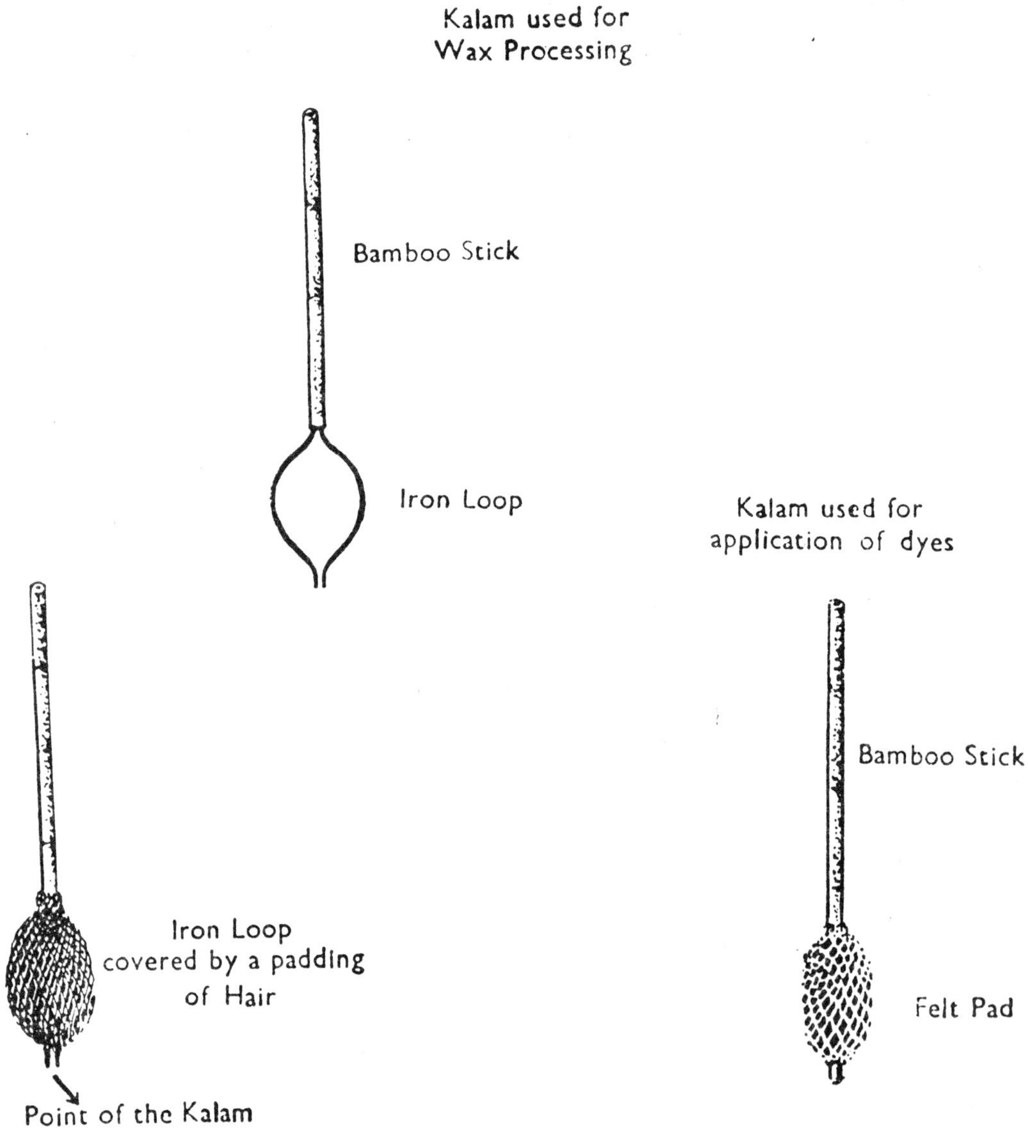
Kalam used for
Wax Processing
Bamboo Stick
Iron Loop
Kalam used for
application of dyes
Bamboo Stick
Iron Loop
covered by a padding
of Hair
Felt Pad
Point of the Kalam

Fig. 3. Kalams.

1. Initial preparation of cloth
2. Outline Block Printing
3. Wax Processing
4. Blue Dyeing
5. Yellow Dyeing
6. Finishing

The Stage No. 1 : is preparing the cloth for Kalamkari process. The mill-made Kora long cloth is used as the basic material over which Kalamkari work is carried out. The Kora is a kind of rough unbleached long cloth usually light brownish in colour and un-starched. Before this cloth is utilized for Kalamkari processing it has to be cleaned and bleached white. For this purpose, an indigenous method of bleaching (without using any chemicals), has been evolved at Masulipatnam. The kora long cloth which is cut to the required sizes is soaked in goat or buffalo dung solution in a big pot, through-out the night and the next morning it is cleaned in the flowing water of river and canal and then dried on the water weeds. This bleaching process is repeated for four or five days till the cloth becomes spotless white.

The Stage No. 2 : is mordanting of the bleached cloth in myrobalan solution for taking up the block printing. The cloth is dipped into a solution made from myrobalan fruit and fresh buffalo milk and uniformly soaked and then dried. After this mordanting process, the cloth becomes yellowish in appearance.

The Stage No. 3 : is Block printing i.e., the printing of the outlines of the design. The outlines are printed either in black or in red or a combination of both. The black and red printing dye is also manufactured by the blocks which are engraved on the teak wood pieces of convenient sizes. Having decided on the particular design and selected the blocks, the outline printing is done. The black colour is called *Kasam* and the red colour is called *Karam* by the Kalamkari workers. The *Kasam and Karam* have to be kept in conveniently large inkpad like structures suited for dipping the printing blocks. For this purpose , wooden trays made of deodar or teakwood are prepared, into which bamboo separators are introduced breadth wise. Over these, flannel, felt or cotton cloth padding is spread. Now the tray-cum-printing pad is ready to take the required printing colour. With the printing blocks selected and the printing pads with the required colour-black or red, by his side, the worker proceeds to print the outlines. For convenience of block printing, a dyeing table is used. The block printer sits by the side of the low table and attends to the printing. The outline designs so printed are usually floral or made up of animals and birds.

The Stage No. 4 : After the block printing, the cloth is allowed to dry in the sun. After two or three days it is taken and cleaned in running water and then dried on waterweeds.

The Stage No. 5 : is Scalding. This process is intended to give permanent red colour to the outlines printed. It also helps to remove the gum and myrobalan juice from the cloth.

The Stage No. 6 : is Bleaching. This process is same as described in stage 1. Through the bleaching process, excepting the areas where black and red outlines are printed the rest of the area is rendered white.

The Stage No. 7 : Starching : Rice starch is prepared and the starch solution is taken out in a separate container and the cloth is soaked in it and then dried by spreading it on grass.

The Stage No. 8 : is Wax processing : This is the important process, which distinguishes the Kalamkari printing of Masulipatnam from other common dyeing industry. It is in the course of this important stage of the processing of the fabric that all characteristic implements of Kalamkari industry are brought in to use. But the most important requirement is an earthen pot or for convenience sake a half broken pot forming a shallow basin. The hearth is prepared with the help of three bricks with paddy husk placed in the middle of it. The husk is not allowed to burn into a flame but the fire is kept going without the flame. The earthen pot basin is put on this husk with bee wax in it. The bee wax melts and the low heat of the hearth keeps the wax in a molten state but without unduly raising its temperature. The molten wax should be only of a suitable consistency so that it can be conveniently applied on to the cloth. The Kalamkari worker by his experience knows what consistency has to be maintained. The molten wax is thus kept ready and the workers sit round it with work benches and the starched outline printed cloth spread over it with the Kalams in their hands. The Kalam is dipped in the molten wax. The pad absorbs the liquid wax. The workers by exerting gentle pressure on the pad make the wax run down the points of the Kalam and thus apply it to the cloth over all the required areas leaving aside those portions of the cloth which have to be dyed blue. The molten wax covers all the rest. This wax covering is necessary in order to see that blue dyeing that is done under the next stage does not spread on to portions covered by the wax. The cloth covered by the molten wax is put in the sun for a little while till the wax film shows signs of melting. This is considered necessary so that any gaps not effectively covered by the Kalam may be got automatically filled by this spreading of the wax film when it melts under the sun. The women workers at their homes attend to this wax covering process.

The Stage No. 9 : The next stage is blue dyeing. The special blue dyeing process is a matter of prestige to the traditional Kalamkari worker. The blue dye is prepared very carefully by making use of natural vegetable colour obtained from the indigo plant, which is grown extensively in the neighouring Taluk of Divi and also in Jaggayyapet and Nandigama Taluks of the Krishna District.

After the blue dye is prepared, the wax covered cloth which is neatly folded is then dipped in the dye solution and kept in it for a few minutes and then taken out and hung on a bamboo pole. The cloth has to be examined to see whether it has taken up the blue colour uniformly, if not, it should be dipped again. The cloth is then spread out resting it on pegs. Even at this stage, if any areas are found not adequately dyed, the blue dye solution can be applied on the cloth by using soft brush.

The Stage No. 10 : is Wax Removal: After the blue dyeing process is finished, the cloth has now got to be relieved of the wax covering so that it may be put through the other dyeing process. For this purpose the cloth is put in a big copper vessel and boiled. The molten wax comes out of the cloth. The cloth is then removed and dried in order to take out all traces of wax on the cloth, with the help of a spoon made out of coconut shell. The entire wax removed can once again be utilized for wax processing.

The Stage No. 11 : Cleaning and bleaching of the Cloth:

After the removal of the molten wax the cloth has got to be cleaned and bleached. The Kalamkari worker prefers a cleaning agent without any alkali.

The Stage No. 12 : Starching : After the cloth is cleaned subsequent to the blue dyeing, it has to be once again starched. The process is same as mentioned in the Stage-7 While starching, buffalo milk is also added, which is said to prevent the colours from spreading out when dyeing.

The Stage No. 13 : is Dyeing the cloth yellow and green : We have so far seen that the Kalamkari cloth has taken the outline designs in black and red some interspaced dyed blue. The remaining colours that are usually applied to the Kalamkari designs are yellow and green. The yellow colouring material is also a vegetable dye obtained by boiling myrobalan flowers in water. This yellow colour is applied on the Kalamkari cloth spread on the low work benches, by means of a small Kalam different from that used for waxing process and it is made up of a mere bamboo stick with felt tied in the middle. The Kalam is dipped in the yellow colour and by exerting pressure on the felt whenever needed. The felt is also useful for blotting back any excess dye that may flow out of the Kalam. The areas to be coloured green are already dyed blue. The yellow myrobalan colour is applied on these portions so that a green colour is evolved at the required places.

The Stage No. 14 : is the finishing stage, which is Application of Alum solution : With the application of yellow colour, the dyeing processes are almost all complete. The colours so applied are all now confirmed and made all permanent by dipping the cloth in alum solution. The cloth is then dried in the sun for a day. The cloth is then dipped in hard water for about half an hour and then soaked in cow dung solution and wronged and tied up into a bundle and kept away for a night. Then it is washed in a river and dried over waterweeds. The process is repeated another night. This gives the yellow colour brightness. Ultimately the cloth is boiled and washed with soap by which the colours are brought out in their full lustre.

With this long, laborious and somewhat complicated process of bringing out the Kalamkari fabric of Masulipatnam is completed. It is said that it would take about two months for a piece of cloth to undergo all these processes and come out as a finished product. At present the Kalamkari work is being carried on at centres in Masulipatnam town viz., at (i) Balyalagudem Kalamkari Works, Desaipeta, Bandar, and (ii) Rekapalli Parthasarathy Kalamkari Works, Rustumbada, and Bandar.

Designs :

The designs and the varieties of the Kalamkari printed fabric of Masulipatnam had been evolved originally to meet three types of demands, (1) For export to Persia and other Middle-Eastern countries (2) For export to Western countries, and (3) For meeting domestic consumption.

The products exported to the Middle-Eastern countries consisted of bed-sheets, Curtains, Tents, Prayer cloth etc., for which typical Persian design are adopted for printing. These varieties bear the following names of Persian or Arabic derivation: Gulabadami, Guleheli, Cherangmorkmath, Gulebachadar Bagal, Janemaz.

The products intended for export to the Western countries like the U.K, the U.S.A, France and Germany consisted of palang-posh or bed-sheets, door-curtains table cloths etc. For this variety floral and animal designs are generally adopted. Of late, cloth by the yard with small design of flowers or leaves printed called "Chintz" is also being produced for export.

The third category intended for domestic consumption and also for export to Far-Eastern countries like Sri Lanka, Singapore etc., consisted of varieties of sarees, with and without borders and wide pallus. Some have great varieties of border designs. A few popular designs are muthyala pandiri, gandabherunda or double bird design. Borders of table cloths and curtains with figures of horses, elephants, camels, swans, parrots are also quite common.

At present, the Kalamkari printers of Masulipatnam Town are divided into two broad groups. One group wants to follow only the traditional method of Kalamkari production. And the second group has taken to the production of the art by using chemical dyes, which are cheaper when compared to the vegetable dyes. However, the products are inferior to the traditional ones. But one finds it difficult to distinguish the cloth prepared under the two processes. Because sometimes the Kalamkari cloth prepared using the chemical dyes looks even more attractive as the chemical dyes appear brighter than the vegetable dyes. But it is obvious that they can never have the keeping qualities of the vegetable dyes. It is claimed that even if an old Kalamkari cloth may come to the stage of tearing away by its age, the original dye never fades away. It is the traditional wax processing and the vegetable colour dyeing which gave the industry its fame. Therefore, it is not most important that the traditional process should be preseverd.

The Kalamkari industry was badly affected for several reasons. The stoppage of imports of the products into Persia in the year 1930 was one of the main reasons. The fine pieces that were produced for the Persian market ceased to be produced. The industrial Revolution of the west had also hit the Masulipatnam industry badly. The other reasons were the industrialization of the textile industry within the country, the competition from the cheaper mill products of the present day are far inferior to those that were the pride of the industry a few decades ago. At this stage, one can hope that with the present demand not only with in our country but even outside for artistic products produced by traditional craftsmen. The Kalamkari industry may once again come to its original form and fame.

C. Woollen Pile Carpet Industry

Pile Carpets were probably introduced in India from Iran. The earliest reference to them is found in 15th century, when their export to other countries was mentioned in the travelogies of the period. Detailed references to the pile carpet industry were found in Ain-I-Akbari. During the Mughal period, this industry flourished in Agra, Delhi, and Lahore as also in the Deccan.

There are two centres in Andhra Pradesh noted for the woollen pile carpet industry, viz., Eluru and Warangal [Plate No. 15]

Warangal : This historic city is an important district headquarters of Andhra Pradesh lying at a distance of about 151

Kms. Northeast of the State capital, Hyderabad. The pile carpet industry for which this place earned a name appears to have been introduced by the local Muslim nawabs. The industry was obviously borrowed from Persia. The Warangal pile carpet industry cannot trace its origin because there is no recorded evidence of how this industry was first introduced into Warangal. It is interesting to find that the looms, the technique of production, the tools, the original designs are almost the exact replicas of those found in Persia. And also, the pile carpet weavers are almost entirely the Muslims. It is well known that during the reign of the Qutub Shahis of Golconda there was free trade carried between this part of the country and the Middle Eastern countries, and this industry seems to have been borrowed into Warangal under the partronage of the local Nawabs. With its technique already developed in Persia the industry appears to have been introduced into Warangal for no other reason but the availability of wool, the chief raw material, from tanneries and also because of the luxury loving nawabs who placed regular orders for the pile carpets, mostly prayer carpets of size 4"×2" and a set design were being manufactured here and supplied to the Muslim nobility.

The Warangal pile carpets soon established a name for themselves. They were able to secure a good foreign market in the West. It is said that generally carpets of size 7'×4' were being exported to an extent of about the 10,000 pieces per month. The industry at its peak was providing employment to about 500 craftsmen.

Later on, the demand for the Warangal carpet in the foreign market died down. But no specific reasons are revealed for the failure of the carpet factory. However, it so happened that, in order to earn some quick profits some of the greedy capitalists introduced some inferior material (sagarmatta fibre) instead of jute in the manufacture of the carpet. This inferior material is not long lasting and becomes brittle and breaks when the carpet is folded. Hence the demand in the foreign market came down. As a result, several workers were thrown out of employment. They took to alternative occupations to eke out their livelihood. In the year 1930-31 a Government Carpet Factory was started to rehabilitate these workers. But was closed down after about 15 or 16 years. Some of the old workers, who had knowledge of its existence, attribute the failure to financial break-down.

In 1952 the Warangal Cottage and Small Scale Industries Co-operative Society Limited, Warangal was started with 177 members. The society could start its production of pile carpets only in 1955. But there are some craftsmen who were actively engaged in this industry outside the Co-Operative Society. But some of the well-known craftsmen have either left the industry altogether or some are now dead.

At present, there may not be more than 30-40 workers who have this industry as their source of livelihood.

The *Raw Material* and *Implements* needed for woollen pile carpet manufacture are as follows :

1. Wool.
2. Jute Twine and cotton twine for binding (Weft).
3. Cotton yarn (for the Warp).
4. Dyes-Chemical dyes-only acid colours are required as wool takes these colours only.
5. Dyeing vats for dying wool.
6. Stillages for drying dyed woollen yarn.
7. Loom.
8. (a) A special knife.
   (b) Reed or comb beater.
   (c) Scissors.

Carpet Designs

The old traditional designs of the Warangal carpets are as follows :

1. Hashim Khani
2. Delhi Khani
3. Teerandas Khani
4. Mahbub Khani
5. Thotti Designs

These are all Persian designs said to consume a lot of labour. Originally prayer carpet called "Jahnamaz" of size 4'×2' with the design of a rectangular figure with a dome at a top, was being produced. Of late the centre has taken to the production of any modern design with floral or geometrical figures as per the orders given or made by the customers. The floral motifs have acquired more demand these days.

Manufacturing Process

The customer wanting to produce a carpet indicates the design of the carpet because the carpet production centre does not maintain any catalogue except an album showing few designs. The carpet manufacturer can produce the carpet of any given design. Therefore the consumer with individual tastes prefer to give their own design. On a customer indicating the design, it is reduced on to a graph sheet in which the colours are also noted.

By examining the design and the colour scheme, and taking into consideration the size of the carpet and the texture, the quantity of woollen yarn needed and the colours into which it should be dyed are determined.

Raw wool is obtained in four colours, namely, White, Black,

Fawn and Grey. These are spun into yarn. The white woollen yarn, which cost more, is used for obtaining all light colours only by dyeing. The fawn coloured wool is used for being dyed into maroon, green, brown, red or blue colours. Grey wool is used for being dyed into very dark colours such as dark red, dark green etc. Sometimes a mixture of different shades of natural coloured wool, such as grey and white is made and dyed to produce certain intermediate colour. The dyeing of wool is also a specialized process. Only the chemical dyes available in the market are used for this purpose. Chemical dyes are preferred because it is felt that once when the yarn takes the chemical dye it is free form moth attack.

After finalizing the design and securing the required quantity of woollen yarn of the requisite colours as also the cotton yarn and the jute weft thread, the first stage of manufacture consist of the tying of required warp. Strong cotton thread is required for the warp.

The pile carpet loom is an interesting contrivance constructed with indigenous materials. The loom is erected along side a long low trench of about 2' deep and about 2' wide. The length of the trench depends upon the size of loom that is erected. They range from 4' to 18'. On either end of the trench are erected two vertical strong wooden posts of about 9" diameter and 9' high with a fork at the top. Babul or Neem wooden posts are preferred as they will be heavy, strong and will not be easily affected by white ants. The 'Y' fork at the top support a horizontal wooden roller. A wooden roller 9" in diameter is put across the vertical posts on the top and another similar wooden roller is mounted across the vertical supports at the foot just above the trench. The top roller has a number of pegs for holding the warp when mounted. The bottom roller has a groove into which the bamboo carrying the warp can be fitted in. Both these horizontal rollers have tensioning levers with the help of which the warp can be rolled or unrolled and the required tension of warp threads maintained.

When the warp is mounted on to the loom it will be vertical. The worker sits in front of the bottom roller of the loom with his feet inside the trench. Next the prepared warp is mounted on the loom, one end around the top roller of the loom and the other end fixed in the groove of the bottom roller. The threads of the warp are then adjusted and tied to form the required number of knots per inch.

Next, the main process of weaving of the carpet begins : The worker sits in the front of the mounted vertical loom with the woollen yarn of the required colours wound in to spherical balls which are hung along a horizontal rod behind him. It is a narrow carpet of about 3' or 4' wide a single worker can handle the loom by himself. If it is a wider carpet to be prepared, then a number of workers work together sitting along the pit so that each has to attend to about 2' or 3' width of the carpet. When a team of workers attend to this work, there will be a head weaver who will be in charge of the design sheet and for each time he calls out the pattern.

The forming of knots is an interesting process during the weaving of the carpet. For this, the worker gets hold of the end of woollen yarn of the required colour from the balls of woollen yarn that are kept hanging behind him and takes it across the warp threads dexterously by winding it round the threads in an alternative fashion and forms a knot. Soon after the knot is so made, the worker cuts the ends of the woollen yarn with the special knife and the knot is made. After the knotting of the yarn over the entire row is completed, the binding thread, which will form the weft, is passed through the warp. The warp threads are then leased by moving the bent wooden bits, which are placed just above the head of the worker on the loom. The binding jute yarn is once again passed through and the wrap threads are again leased and then lastly the cotton binding thread called bafa is passed and the warp leased for the third time. The worker strikes down the pile and the binding threads together each time the binding weft is passed through the wrap with a reed (Panja). The pile ends are then cut uniformly by the worker with an ordinary scissors to maintain a common level. Thus a team of workers keep on weaving the carpet line by line by a process of knotting the pile, binding, leasing and securing the pile firmly by beating down with the reed and finally cutting the pile till the entire length of the carpet is completed. As and when the carpet piling keeps making progress the bottom roller of the loom is wound with the woven carpet.

After the weaving of carpet on the loom is completed and is dismounted from the loom, it is spread on the floor and the piles are given a final leveling up by shearing it with finishing scissors. The ends of the carpet are knotted and the carpet given a general brushing. The carpet is now ready for the market.

Though this industry had at one time enjoyed considerable reputation, it suffered a great set back in the recent past and the plight of workers became pitiable. They had mostly taken up to alternate occupations.

The industry is at present depending on the fortunes of the Co-Operative Society formed in 1952. The Society received considerable assistance from the All India Handicrafts Board. With the encouragement given by the All India Handicrafts Board and the Industries Department of the State Government the pile carpet industry of Warangal seems to recapture its past glory. Standardization of the designs, production of a catalogue and price list, adequate publicity and advertisement would help to push up the demand for the articles produced.

Woollen pile carpet Industry of Eluru

Eluru, the district headquarters town of West Godavari district is renowned for its woolen pile carpet industry.

There is no recorded evidence of how and when the carpet industry came to be started in this town. It is obvious that it was not indigenous but introduced from outside. It is believed to be the result of the Mughal rule over this part of the country. The local workmen relate that several hundreds of years ago the Mughal army happened to encamp in the area over the ground locally known as Lashmivarapupet. It is said that a couple of Persians amongst the camping troops stayed back in the Tangellamudi on the outskirts, which now forms part of Eluru town. It seems that these two persons knew the art of Persian carpet weaving and since the local weavers and dyers were specialists in the vegetable dyeing, this seemed to have encouraged the new settlers to start a pile carpet industry using the local dyes. The shepherd families' residing in the neighbourhood readily supplied the wool. In Tangellamudi the population of Muslim community who ran tanneries was considerably high. Thus the environment and availability of raw material seems to have proved propitious for the development of the pile carpet industry. Soon, most the Muslim families residing here picked up the craft. Most of the individual families had small looms in their homes, and with the simple technique involved and the limited implements needed it was easy for the local workmen to develop a skill in the making of the pile carpets, which soon won a wide reputation.

The pile carpet manufacturing units of Eluru are located in Tangellamudi and Lakshmivarapupet.

As for the technique of manufacture, the type of looms and the implements used are almost identical to those employed at Warangal.

Designs

In the Eluru carpets, the designs are attractive with beautiful colours. They generally comprise of the traditional Persian and

Mughal patterns, though modern designs have also been adopted. The following are some of the most famous designs.

In the traditional category we have the Ramachanderkhani, Poshkhani, Lolakhani, (actually Lovelock khani), Camel foot, Gulabkani, Jaipur, Nurjehan, Taj Khani, Hashimkhani, Sherkhani etc. The Reddi design seems to be a popular modern design. Though the design as such is standardized, colour scheme seems to vary from one carpet to another. At Eluru, no symbolic significance is attached to the various designs of the carpets. But a few types are associated with religious practice e.g., the carpets with Janemaz design are taken by Muslims for performing their daily prayers.

It is seen that there are more number of designs in vogue at Eluru than at Warangal. The reason commonly given out for the flourishing of more number of designs at Eluru is that there are by far larger number of working craftsmen at Eluru, who could produce several new models by the dexterous combination of parts from two or more existing designs. Beside this, Eluru has a regular foreign trade.

CHAPTER - V

CONCLUSION

The above study, will no doubt give an idea of the magnificence of our textile tradition. The range and variety of Indian fabrics is immense. Every technique and every mode, from the simplest to the most complicate, have been practiced for centuries and in every class. There are the artistic forms and designs, which have received, unstained admiration the world over. Broadly speaking, the patterns and designs in all types of Indian fabrics display an instinctive sense of proportion, a rhythmic harmony of line and curve and sensitive eye for colour.

Unfortunately, decadence has set in and most of the traditional forms are long past their days of splendor. The impact of foreign rule and the consequent changes in fashions and tastes have no doubt proved disastrous to every indigenous industry. The machine has supplanted the handloom, which was the main stay of beautiful textile forms. However, the innate genius and skill of the traditional craftsmen still exists, and what is required more than anything else is a change in outlook, which enable one to love, understand and cherish one's own artistic heritage.

Recently there has been a remarkable growth in the handloom industry primarily as a result of the initiative of the weaving community. Pupul Jayakar opines that "The unique skill of the weaver, his comprehension of colour, texture and function, the weaver's capacity for rapid adaptation and for production of small yardage in a variety of designs" has been the industry's greatest strength. Handloom cloth has become an important foreign exchange earner on account of its ability to meet the needs of fashion market, producing even a hundred meters of fabric in a particular design or colour combination to meet the individual taste of the consumer. It is this exclusiveness of handloom that gives it an edge over cloth produced by the other sectors.

It is necessary to continue research on improving the quality and productivity of handlooms. Studies have shown that minor modifications in machines and processes can increase productivity up to 50%. The textile policy statement of 1985 recognized the distinct and unique role of the handloom sector and proposed a number of measures for the preservation and growth of this sector as one of the priority areas in the country's development program. One of the most important of these is the introduction of technical innovations in the loom used by the weavers, so as to increase the productivity and improve the quality of the product.

Other supportive measures have been undertaken by the government, in addition to an active program of supply of materials, worksheds, common facilities etc. to be carried out through cooperatives and State corporations. The existing marketing structure is being strengthened and an intensive program for publicity and promotion has been launched to expand local and export markets. A census of handlooms is being carried out to broaden the database. This would help in better planning and programming of development programs. Recommendations were also made in training and upgrading of the technical, managerial and administrative skills of the handloom sector.

With these measures, the handloom sector is expected to be greatly strengthened and many of the inadequacies that have existed in the system are expected to overcome.

BOOKS CONSULTED

Census of India, 1961, Vol. II, Part VII-A (1), Delhi, 1964.

Census of India, 1961, Vol. II, Part VII-A (2), Delhi, 1965.

Census of India, 1961, Vol. II, Part VII-A (3), Delhi, 1967.

Homage to Kalamkari, Marg Publication, Bombay, Vol. xxxi.

Jasleen Dhamija & Jyotindra Jain (Ed.), *Hand Woven Favbrics of India.*USA, 1989.

Saraswati, S.K., *Indian Textiles,* Faridabad, 1961.

Suguna Sharma, V., *Studies In Indian Textiles,* New Delhi 1998.

Treasures of Indian Textiles, Calico Museum, Ahmedabad, Marg Publication, Bombay, 1980.

INDEX

Y

Z

✦✦✦

Pl. 1. Pochampally Silk saree (Traditional)

Pl. 2. Pochampally Silk saree (Traditional)

Pl. 3. Pochampally Silk saree–Single side border.

Pl. 4. Pochampally Cotton saree–double border.

Pl. 5. Gadwal saree with double border

Pl. 6. Dharmavaram Silk saree with double side border.

Pl. 7. Kanchipuram Silk saree with double side border.

Pl. 8. Kanchipuram Silk saree with double side border.

Pl. 9. Patur Silk saree.

Pl. 10. Patur Silk saree.

Pl. 11. Narayanpet silk saree.

Pl. 12. Venkatagiri cotton saree.

Pl. 13. Himroo Silk.

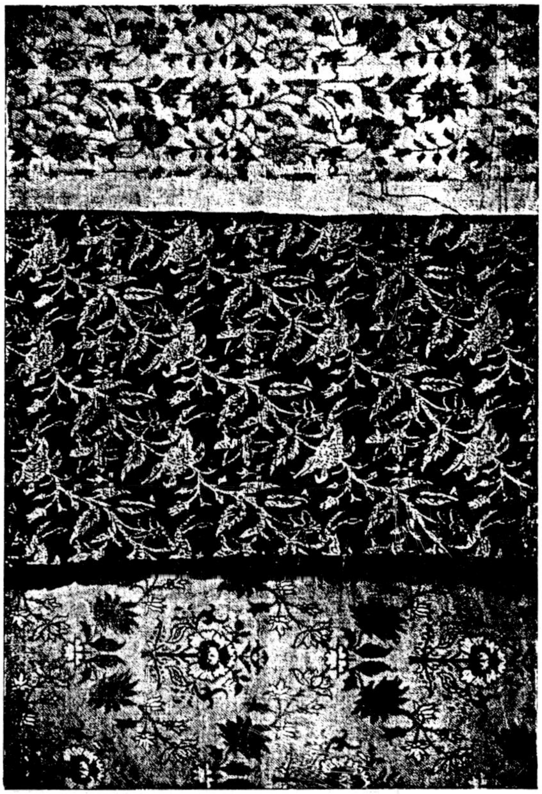

Pl. 14. Himroo Silks-For dressing Gowns; Sher-wani; Curtains. etc

Pl. 15. Carpets.